Indira Nehru Gandhi

INDIRA NEHRU GANDHI
Ruler of India

by Carol Greene

CHILDRENS PRESS™
CHICAGO

PHOTO CREDITS

AP/Wide World—9, 17 (left), 19, 20, 21, 22 (2 photos), 23 (2 photos), 24 (2 photos), 28, 30 (3 photos)

The Bettmann Archive—13

Black Star/© Max Scheler—Cover, 2, 6
© Milt and Joan Mann—26

UPI/Bettman Archive—8, 11, 15, 16, 17 (right), 25, 27, 29 (2 photos), 31

Len Meents—art, 14

Cover: Indira Gandhi

Library of Congress Cataloging in Publication Data

Greene, Carol.
    Indira Nehru Gandhi, ruler of India.

    (Picture-story biographies)
    Summary: Describes how Indira Gandhi followed her family's tradition of fighting politically for India, became prime minister, and was assassinated by her enemies.
    1. Gandhi, Indira, 1917-1984—Juvenile literature.
2. Prime ministers—India—Biography—Juvenile literature.
[1. Gandhi, Indira, 1917-1984. 2. Prime ministers. 3. India—Politics and government—20th century]
I. Title. II. Series.
DS481.G23G74   1985   954.04'5 0924 [B] [92] 85-359
ISBN 0-516-03478-2

INDIRA NEHRU GANDHI

Ruler of India

Indira visiting schoolchildren in India.

"India comes first." All her life Indira Nehru Gandhi heard that message. She believed it, too.

For many years Great Britain ruled India. The Indian people grew tired of that. They wanted to be free to rule themselves.

Indira's grandfather, Motilal (MOH•tih•lahl) Nehru, worked for India's freedom. So did her father, Jawaharlal (juh•WAH•hur•lahl) Nehru, and her mother, Kamala Nehru. So did a great leader called

Rashtrapati Jawaharlal Nehru (left), Indira's father, was India's first prime minister. He served from 1947 to 1964. He supported the principles of Mohandas Gandhi (right).

Mohandas Gandhi. He was a good friend of the Nehru family. Gandhi was a good friend of India, too. He believed that by following the principles of courage, truth, and nonviolence India would win her freedom from Great Britain.

Baby Indira with her mother, Kamala, and her father, Jawaharlal

Indira was born November 19,
1917, in her grandfather's house in
Allahabad. That is in the province
of Kashmir in northern India. Her
grandfather's house was called
Anand Bhavan (House of Joy).

But it was not always a joyful place for little Indira. Her family loved her, but they were also busy with politics. So Indira often felt lonely.

Sometimes her family went to jail because of their work for India's freedom. Her father, mother, grandfather, grandmother, aunts, and uncles all spent time in jail. Then Indira felt sad.

Indira wanted to work for India, too. When she was still very small, she would stand on a table in the garden and make speeches. The servants and their children were her audience.

Gandhi was India's hero. The people called Gandhi the
Mahatma, which means Great Soul.

Once Mohandas Gandhi said that
Indians should use only Indian
things. Indira's family agreed. They
burned all their British things. Indira
looked at her doll. She loved her
doll, but it was British. So she
burned it.

Indira's father and grandfather led
a political group called the Indian
National Congress party. When
Indira was eleven, she wanted to
join.

"No," she was told. "You must wait until you are eighteen."

So Indira started a children's group. She called it the Monkey Brigade. More than a thousand children joined. They ran errands and helped the grown-ups in the Congress party.

Indira went to many different schools—even one in Switzerland. She loved to read and her father gave her all the books she wanted. In 1934 she went to a special university called Visva-Bharati. There she learned about Indian arts and about nature. It was a happy time for Indira.

But in 1935 she had to leave school. Her mother was very ill with tuberculosis. Her father was in prison. So Indira went with her

Oxford University

mother to doctors in Switzerland.
There, in 1936, Kamala Nehru died.

After that, Indira went to
England. She studied at Somerville
College, Oxford University. Again
she felt happy. But she felt
homesick, too. There was so much
work to be done in India!

Then came World War II. For a
while Indira worked as an
ambulance driver for the British Red
Cross. But in 1941 she went home to
India. With her went a young man
named Feroze Gandhi. He was not
related to Mohandas Gandhi. But he
was a good friend of the Nehru
family.

Indira Gandhi talks with her son and political heir, Rajiv.

Indira told her father that she wanted to marry Feroze. At first he didn't like the idea. But he changed his mind. On March 26, 1942, the young people were married. In 1944 they had their first child, a boy named Rajiv. In 1946 their second son, Sanjay, was born. Meanwhile, both Indira and Feroze Gandhi went on working for India's freedom.

Dr. P. P. Pillai, India's representative to the United Nations, raises the flag of Free India at U.N. headquarters in New York.

At last, in 1947, India became an independent country. There were many problems. Other countries fought with India. The Indian people fought with one another. Many, many Indians were very poor. But now India had a strong prime minister—Indira's father, Jawaharlal Nehru.

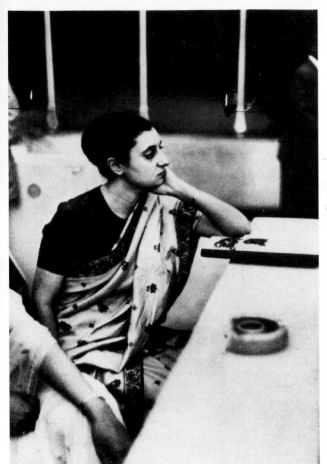

Indira Gandhi (left) attended many political meetings for her father.
Prime Minister Nehru (right) reviews the troops.

Indira Gandhi knew her father
needed a lot of help. She did all she
could for him. At last she and her
sons went to live with her father.
This was not good for her marriage
to Feroze. But once again, India
came first.

Indira traveled all over the world with her father. She listened to his problems and helped him give parties and dinners. And all the while she was learning about politics.

In 1955, the Congress party asked her to be on the committee that ran it. In 1959 they asked her to be president of the party. Some people thought she would be a weak president. They were wrong. Indira got rid of people who weren't doing their jobs. She helped party members work together.

Nehru and Indira attended the Afro-Asian Conference in Bandung, Indonesia in 1955.

In 1966 Mrs. Gandhi visited New York State
and met with Governor Nelson Rockefeller (right).

But Jawaharlal Nehru was getting
old. He needed her more and more.
So after a year Indira Gandhi quit
her job as party president to be with
her father.

Then, in 1964, Jawaharlal had a
stroke. Indira became his nurse. She
stayed by his bed and helped him
run the country. But after a few
months, her father died.

After the death of Lal Bahadur Shastri, Indira Gandhi became prime minister and head of the nation's largest political party.

A man named Lal Bahadur Shastri became the prime minister. He asked Indira if she would like a job in the government. She said she would like to be minister of information and broadcasting. But she did not have the job for long.

In 1966 Shastri died. The government leaders had to choose a new prime minister. They soon decided who that should be—Indira Nehru Gandhi.

Indira met with the world's political leaders, such as British Foreign Secretary Sir Alec Douglas-Hume (left) and President Richard Nixon of the United States (right), to seek support for India.

Suddenly she was the ruler of millions of people. Some called her the most powerful woman in the world. But others wondered if she were strong enough for the job.

Indira showed them that she *was* strong. She worked at India's money problems. She helped form the new country of Bangladesh. She won political battles. Most of all, she tried to make the rest of the world see that India was a great power.

In the 1980s Chinese Vice Premier and Foreign Minister Huang Hua (left) and President Ronald Reagan (right) discussed world matters with Mrs. Gandhi.

Then, in 1975, Indira ran into trouble. A court said that she had not won her last election fairly. Other government leaders said she must resign as prime minister. Indira didn't resign. Instead she had those who were against her put in jail. Many people believed she was wrong to do that.

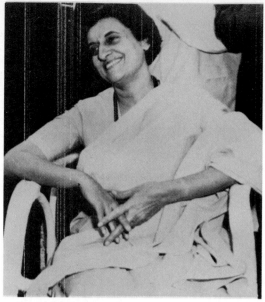

Indira Gandhi did everything she could to defeat her opposition. She did not always win, but she always fought for what she wanted. As a result, she had many enemies.

In 1977 she lost an election. One of the men she had put in jail became prime minister. Now it was Indira's turn to be arrested. She went to jail twice.

But 1980 brought another election. This time Indira won and for the second time became prime minister. Suddenly it seemed as if all India loved her. They called her Madam or Amma (Mother). Sometimes they just called her She. Everyone knew who She was.

Sanjay, Indira's youngest son, was killed in a glider crash in 1980.

But 1980 was a sad time for Indira, too. Her younger son, Sanjay, died when the plane he was flying crashed. Still, Indira could not stop working, no matter how sad she felt. India came first.

Golden Temple in Amritsar, India

A group of people in India wanted to start their own country. They were members of the Sikh religion. Some of them turned their Golden Temple into a fortress. They went out from the temple to force other people to support their plan.

Indira knew this political opposition must end. She ordered soldiers to attack the Golden Temple. Many Sikhs and soldiers died in that battle.

The funeral procession carried the body of Indira Gandhi
through the streets of New Delhi, the capital of India.

But Indira did not think she
should be angry with all Sikhs. That
was not the way to help India live in
peace. She even kept Sikhs as some
of her own guards.

On October 31, 1984, Indira
walked through her garden. She said
hello to two of her Sikh guards. She

Riots broke out following the assassination of Mrs. Gandhi. Hundreds of Sikhs (left) were attacked, and their homes and businesses burned. The army was called out to restore peace.

had known one of them for many years. She trusted them.

But the men wanted revenge for what had happened at their temple. So they shot Indira.

Terrible riots broke out when the Indian people learned that Indira was dead. Many Sikhs were killed. Buildings were burned.

Surrounded by family members the body of Indira Gandhi (above) was cremated in a public ceremony. Wrapped in their country's flag (below right), Indian citizens followed Mrs. Gandhi's funeral procession. Rajiv Gandhi (left) was sworn in as India's prime minister, by president of India Zail Singh.

Indira's son Rajiv became the new prime minister. He begged the people to stop their riots. Such things were not good for India. And Rajiv knew what his mother would say. "India comes first."

INDIRA NEHRU GANDHI

1917	November 19—Born in Allahabad, northern India, only child of Jawaharlal and Kamala Nehru
1934-35	Attended Visva-Bharati, an Indian university
1936	Enrolled at Somerville College, Oxford University, England
1941	Returned to India
1942	Married Feroze Gandhi
1947	Helped her father, who was now prime minister of independent India
1955	Named to administrative committee of Congress party
1959	Chosen president of Congress party
1960	Resigned as president to help her father
1964	Became minister of information and broadcasting
1966	Became prime minister of India
1977	Lost election for prime minister
1980	Reelected prime minister
1984	October 31—Shot and killed by Sikh guards

ABOUT THE AUTHOR

CAROL GREENE has degrees in English Literature and Musicology. She has worked in international exchange programs, as an editor, and as a teacher. She now lives in St. Louis, Missouri, and writes full-time. She has had published over fifty books—most of them for children. Other Childrens Press biographies by Ms. Greene include *Sandra Day O'Connor: First Woman on the Supreme Court* and *Mother Teresa: Friend of the Friendless* in the Picture Story Biography series, and *Louisa May Alcott, Marie Curie,* and *Thomas Alva Edison* in the People of Distinction series.